To All Leaders:
WHO DO YOU
Think
YOU ARE?

WHAT'S IN YOUR DNA?

PRINCIPLES IN
BIBLICAL LEADERSHIP

Dr. Mattie C. Shaw

To All Leaders:
Who Do You Think You Are?
What's in your DNA?
Principles in Biblical Leadership

Copyright © 2019 Mattie C. Shaw

Cover Design: C Marcel Wiggins

Published by MIGMIR Company USA, LLC
All rights reserved. No part of this publication may be reproduced, distributed or transmitted in any form or by any means, without prior written permission. Unless otherwise identified, scripture quotations are from the King James Version of the Bible.

MIGMIR Company USA, LLC

www.migmir.us

For Worldwide Distribution
Printed in the U.S.A.

ISBN: 9780997347779

Library of Congress Control Number: 2019942352

TABLE OF CONTENTS

Acknowledgments. 5

Dedication. 8

Foreword. 10

Preface 11

Introduction 13

Chapter 1   Who are you? 17
What is leadership?
Leadership and relationships
Leaders and their relationships in my family

Chapter 2   Leadership and discipleship 43
Is leadership predestined by God?
Leadership thought and practice
What is discipleship?

Chapter 3   Changing your mindset 55
Who Are you?
Don't give up - God is in control
What's in your DNA?

TABLE OF CONTENTS CONTINUED

Chapter 4   Justification and reconciliation . . . 71
We Are justified by Christ
What is reconciliation?
Reconciling my family relationships

Chapter 5   Are you connected to God? 87
The power of prayer
Faith in God

Chapter 6   Are you aligned with God? 95
Power and authority
Divine deliverance
Finding our balance

Chapter 7 Preparing for destiny 113
Are you equipped and prepared?
Are you ready to serve God?

Conclusion 121
About the Author 127
References 129
Personal Reflections 135

- ACKNOWLEDGMENTS -

First, I want to thank You, Lord, for Your presence in my life for the past 67 years, as You have allowed me to wake up and to see another day, and have inspired me through Your words. I am also grateful and thankful to You for answering my prayers, for Your healing power, for Your blessings to my family, and for Your spiritual guidance in helping me write this book.

I also want to thank Bishop Lewis Q. Fitzpatrick for my apostolic foundation, and for the support he and Mother Fitzpatrick gave to me and my family throughout the years. I will always be grateful.

I especially thank you, Apostle Martin L. Griffin, the Visionary and Founder of Equipping Ministries Fellowship International (EMFI) and Victory Temple International (VTI), for helping me understand my purpose in serving the Kingdom of God, and for equipping, teaching the Word of God, and for supporting, motivating, and encouraging me to develop my God-given gifts and potential in life.

It is because of your teachings of the Gospel of Jesus Christ I preserve this time to develop my vision of becoming an effective leader and a disciple for Christ to help save souls. As you continue to move in your God-given purpose as an Apostle, I pray God will use and protect you wherever He sends you.

I extend my sincere thanks and appreciation to you, Pastor Dr. Deneen Hatcher-Charlton of Victory Temple International (VTI), for your heart of love, inspiration, spiritual advice, and support. I pray God will continue to bless you, as you fulfill your purpose in serving Him and His people.

I give thanks to you, Apostle Dr. Sandra Smith, Senior Pastor of Foundation of The Word Ministries International, for your time, mentorship, and your daily reinforcement of God's Word. I also appreciate your support and encouragement that helped me to finish this book. I pray God will continue to guide and bless you in fulfilling your purpose of saving God's people.

I also want to thank my extended family and friends, for the love and fellowship during our travels, sharing the holidays and times we witnessed God's love in our lasting relationship.

- DEDICATION -

I dedicate my life to You, Father God, Master and King of the Universe, my Lord and Savior Jesus Christ of Nazareth; for Your amazing love and sacrifice. I give You all the praise, honor, and glory for my life.

To my family who means the world to me; my daughter Nichole, my son Michael, and my granddaughters Brittni and Jazmyn, I want to thank you for your love and support in my life of highs and lows. I could not have made it without you. You helped make me strong and have helped me overcome many obstacles, through your encouragement and faith in me. As parents, we are to love, nurture and protect you, even if it means sometimes altering our lives. I will continue to pray for you, and give you all of my love, hugs, and kisses, and will keep you forever safe in my heart.

Jerry, (my husband) who transitioned on May 31, 2001, I thank him for his love for God, and his love and support to me and our family. He have always inspired me to use my talents and gifts; which is why I dedicate my poem in memory of him...

YOU'RE A BREATH OF FRESH AIR

I love the way you smile, and I love your every touch. You're like a breath of fresh air, and I love you very much! As we share our innermost thoughts, while enjoying the life we sought; I can see how much you care for me you're a breath of fresh air!

To hold you and love you, and when we do spend time; each and every moment just stays on my mind. Laughing, crying, and dining, and all the moments we've shared; Is why I looked to hear from you, each day you're a breath of fresh air.

Your charisma and charm have swept me off my feet; you're a breath of fresh air, you make my life complete. You know how to hold me, and will even open my door. You send me flowers and pull my chair; need I say more! Don't know where we are going; just know that we are friends. And we're lovers for life with hopefully no end. No, don't know where we are headed, and I really don't care. Just as long as I can hold on to this breath of fresh air!

Poem Published April 4, 1994

- FOREWORD -

When I think of leadership, I think about a statement by the Queen of England:

"I know of no single formula for success. But over the years I have observed that some attributes of leadership are universal and are often about finding ways of encouraging people to combine their efforts, their talents, their insights, their enthusiasm and their inspiration to work together."
--Queen Elizabeth II

    In this book, Dr. Mattie Shaw found a way to encourage leaders to come together, use their abilities, and God given talents-- which are the tools to make an impact in our lives, communities, and ministries. She reminds us again of the importance of crucial ingredients in the making and maintaining of effective leadership. It is my firm belief that a true leader has also demonstrated their leadership abilities in leading themselves to education, resources, and teams of individuals that will better themselves and provide accountability that their vision, goals, and objectives become a reality.

    By taking us through biblical history and practical principles, we can see the paths and patterns of effective leaders and learn not only from their successes, but also their failures. As you read her words, it will challenge you to find your own thought process to discover who YOU are, and what really may just be in YOUR D.N.A.

Author, Roy Etienne Smith, B.A., M.Ed., PhD
President of the MIGMIR Company & Isaiah University of the Holy Ghost, Daytona Beach, FL

- PREFACE -

Writing this book has inspired me to share my knowledge and experience, in order to equip, lead, and empower people with an understanding and awareness that some people are born to be leaders in different capacities.

"Now ye are the body of Christ, and members in particular. And God hath set some in the church, first apostles, secondarily prophets, thirdly teachers, after that miracles, then gifts of healings, helps, governments, diversities of tongues. Are all apostles? Are all prophets? Are all teachers? Are all workers of miracles? Have all the gifts of healing? Do all speak with tongues? Do all interpret? But covet earnestly the best gifts: and yet shew I unto you a more excellent way"

(1 Cor. 12:27-31)

In Psalms 8:1-9, we can see the level of love God has for man within His creation, and the purpose God has for man's existence on Earth. In this book I want to set the precedent in consideration of sharing the importance of our relationship with God.

I also seek to emphasize the importance of using our gifts and talents for the purpose of becoming effective leaders in teaching others how to move in excellence, as Disciples of Christ.

"O Lord our Lord, how excellent is thy name in all the earth! who hast set thy glory above the heavens. Out of the mouth of babes and sucklings hast thou ordained strength because of thine enemies, that thou mightest still the enemy and the avenger. When I consider thy heavens, the work of thy fingers, the moon and the stars, which thou hast ordained; What is man, that thou art mindful of him? and the son of man, that thou visitest him? For thou hast made him a little lower than the angels, and hast crowned him with glory and honour. Thou madest him to have dominion over the works of thy hands; thou hast put all things under his feet: All sheep and oxen, yea, and the beasts of the field; The fowl of the air, and the fish of the sea, and whatsoever passeth through the paths of the seas. O Lord our Lord, how excellent is thy name in all the earth!"

(Ps.8:1-9)

INTRODUCTION

It is my belief, once you learn "who you are" in Christ, you will gain a distinct level of awareness, no matter the capacity you are chosen to lead. I pray you will have a better understanding of the importance of becoming effective leaders, as were the Disciples of Christ. Therefore, I write this book based on some of my experiences and opinions. My written testimonies supports my claim that God's assignment to mankind is ordained and leadership is sanctioned as a predestined order of God.

"Then said he unto them, Therefore every scribe which is instructed unto the kingdom of heaven is like unto a man that is an householder, which bringeth forth out of his treasure things new and old" (Mat. 13:52)

In addition, I offer scriptural text, information about my family, and our biblical ancestors to show how the leaders who were appointed by God carried out their assignment. Included is a brief history of the research on leadership thought offered by our predecessors. They emphasized the significance of leadership in the family, and in society.

"God has given us the ability to manage our lives and relationships"

CHAPTER ONE

WHO ARE YOU? ARE YOU A LEADER?

What is leadership?

An effective leader recognizes the importance of building solid relationships and spending time focusing on important areas that will build connections with the people they lead. Leaders have a common goal and a consistent purpose when everyone can share the vision and goal of the leader. It is a collaborative relationship to reach their goals together.

To All Leaders: Who Do You Think You Are?

According to the Merriam-Webster's dictionary, the term relationship is generally used to denote family ties. It's also used as a state of connecting or binding participants. Is your leadership effective? How much do you know about the people you lead?

Effective leaders must be equipped to build relationships and create communities. As one of the motivating factors in building relationships, effective leaders inspire people and help guide them in planning for their future.

"And Moses called unto Joshua, and said unto him in the sight of all Israel, Be strong and of a good courage: for thou must go with this people unto the land which the Lord hath sworn unto their fathers to give them; and thou shalt cause them to inherit it" (Deu. 31:7)

Action plans that bring people together and bind them to common causes are keys used in building effective relationships. When building camaraderie, you are leading-- and by having a meaningful relationship, everyone can prepare to work more effectively together. God is an effective leader who has continued to build covenant relationships with mankind throughout history since the creation of Adam.

Leadership and relationships

What does it take to be a "son of God"? What is your relationship with God based upon?

A personal relationship with God begins with knowing and believing who Jesus is and having the ability to identify who we are. God has given us the ability to manage our lives and relationships. This helps facilitate our thinking process and the way we serve Him.

It is by the Spirit of God, self-awareness, use of our skills and talents, and the understanding of morality and immorality, that we learn things. We learn not only from our own experiences, but also by the experiences of others. As leaders, God gives us an opportunity to manage, make decisions, solve problems, and recognize the process of change.

A man often uses religion to define his degree of spirituality; where emotions, traditions, and logic, play integral parts in formulating his idea of having a relationship with God. Definitions of morality and immortality are also entangled into the fabric of his religious cloak. Religion leans heavily upon man's righteous efforts, which often requires diligent service and works, in expectation of earning an eternal reward. However, it is not the order or matter of your religious state, but it is by the grace of God through faith and belief in Christ that will validate our relationship with God and will allow us to receive the gift of God, which is eternal life in the Kingdom.

"For by grace ye are saved through faith; and that not of yourselves: it is the gift of God:" (Eph.2:8)

"But as many as received him, to them gave he power to become the sons of God, even to them that believe on his name:" (John 1:12)

Inevitably, any shortcomings on the part of the individual who has no relationship with God, there may be consequences: disappointment, guilt-- or an unfulfilled relationship with God, where faith is not included in any service to Him. Having a relationship with God consists of not only having faith and belief, but also being aligned with Him.

Alignment includes being obedient to the mandate of doing His will, communing, loving and serving Him by the leading of the Holy Spirit, and by moving in divine purpose. We are appointed to edify, train, and equip the saints by teaching them the gospel of Jesus Christ. We are to prepare them to become Disciples for Christ.

In the beginning, Adam was chosen to wisely manage everything God breathed life into. Since man was designed to have a relationship, God created Eve as a companion to Adam, and to experience an intimate union and relationship with him. However, Adam failed to uphold his assignment as a leader who would manage that which God created. Unfortunately, he chose to reject and disobey God's command and instructions. He instead yielded to the transgression of sin. Adam separated himself from his relationship with God. The separation resulted in shame and judgment by God towards mankind (Genesis 4). This instance brought many sins, iniquity, and broken relationships between God and man throughout the land.

Restoring our relationship with God may bring the question, Why would an omnipotent and supreme God want a relationship with us?

God chose to create us for a special [purposeful] relationship before the creation of the world (Ephesians 1:4-5). It is His purpose (through His Son Jesus Christ), to prepare us for eternal life in His Kingdom. God does not lie. He made a covenant to bless mankind with everlasting life. What He began in the past He intends to accomplish and complete in the future.

God is our Heavenly Father and He considers us as His children (2 Corinthians

6:16-18).

When He redeemed us, we became sealed into a special relationship with Him. While sin once dominated us to the point of fear and mistrust, as believers in Jesus, we were adopted, and received the same privileges. Christians can now approach God through an intimate relationship with Him.

"The Spirit Himself bears witness with our spirit that we are children of God"

(Rom. 8:16)

We were bought with a special price, "by the precious blood of Jesus Christ" (1 Peter 1:19)

God values us as precious treasures, capable of honoring Him and being holy by the Spirit of God.

It is God's will to save us. When Jesus Christ died on the cross, the divine purpose for Christ's sacrificial death and resurrection from the grave was a plan from God for man's restoration and reconciliation to receive eternal life (Romans 5:12, I Peter 3:18).

Jesus was the only begotten Son of the Father. The relationship they shared while Jesus was on earth is matchless (John 1:14; 6:46; I John 4:9). Through Jesus Christ, we experience God's presence and the strengthening of our relationship through the gifts of the Spirit; with love, faithfulness, sacrifice, mercy, peace, and joy to last throughout eternity.

As leaders, when we draw nearer to Jesus Christ we have an opportunity to change, move closer to God, and serve Him according to His will.

As effective leaders, we learn how to serve in order to bring souls into the Kingdom of God. We strive for spiritual perfection and prepare others to receive the promise of eternal life.

For God so loved the world, that he gave his only begotten Son, that whosoever believeth in him should not perish, but have everlasting life" (John 3:16)

Jesus is changeless because He is God (John 10:30). He is the same yesterday, today, and forever. Forever is an eternal place where God wants us to be. It will be up to us to make that change!

Covenant relationships by God began when God gave man dominion over all the Earth and over everything in it (Genesis 1:26-28). What was God's purpose in giving man dominion? What was the reason God gave Adam such authority and power over all that He created? Did Adam understand the authority God had given him? Did Adam understand the love God had for him? These are questions we must ask. God gave Adam and Eve guidelines to follow. He gave them a choice to either have fellowship and to walk with Him or, walk without Him.

It was not a matter of eating from the tree. It was the importance of obeying and doing God's will. It was also a matter of showing love and respect, devotion, and the value Adam and Eve put in their relationship with God. However, because they wanted to walk on their own, turn to iniquity, and be disobedient to God, their decisions brought on more transgression and wickedness throughout the land.

As sin continued to increase by growing generations, God became grieved and disappointed with His creation. He decided to curse the Earth with a great flood (Genesis 6:1-7). Noah was a faithful man who lived a righteous and blameless life. Thus, God gave Noah an assignment.

God warned Noah about His plan to destroy the earth with a great rain. He instructed Noah to build an ark. Noah never saw rain, but he was obedient and followed God's instructions step by step. In spite of what others (naysayers) had to say, the ark was built and completed after filling it with animals, according to God's instructions. As a result of Noah's obedience, he was able to save his family. After the rain, God replenished the earth and blessed Noah and his family (Genesis 6-8). Thus, their relationship became greater.

God made a covenant with Noah by a sign of the rainbow in the sky, that He would not repeat this act of destruction by water on the earth, again. Afterward, Noah became a just man and an effective leader who walked with God and found grace in His eyes. Then, God blessed Noah to be fruitful and to multiply and replenish the earth (Genesis 9:1-17).

Accordingly, there were about ten generations between the days God made Adam and the day Noah entered the ark to ride out the great flood. The Bible speaks of many leaders and great men who were chosen by God and were direct ancestors of Noah.

To name a few, there were: Enoch who lived 365 years. He had distinctive spirituality and walked with God for 300 years. Enoch was the father of Methuselah, who watched his grandson Noah build the ark. He lived 969 years and was the oldest living human in the Bible. Methuselah's son was Lamech (who lived 777 years).

Lamech was the father of Noah (Genesis 5:21, 25; 4:17, 5:1; 5:21; 4:18, 5:25).

More information on the history about these men can be found in (Genesis 8, Hebrews 11, 2 Peter 2, Ephesians 6, 2 Corinthians 10, and Matthew 12). By the age of 500, Noah had three sons who were named Shem, Ham, and Japheth.

As Noah's sons continued to grow and spread throughout the land, there came the days of Abram who was a descendant of Noah's firstborn, Shem. In his generation were born the children of Israel (the Jewish nation). Abram was a highly regarded leader in the land, but he worshiped idols and involved himself in other evil influences, until he realized who God was and commenced to change his ways.

Afterwards, Abram became a righteous man. When his faith was tested by God, he was told to offer up his son as a sacrifice. It was because of Abram's faith and belief in God, that grace fell upon him, and God placed a "ram in the bush" as a sacrifice instead. As their relationship grew, Abram began to honor God and gave up all that he had to become a great leader.

As a man of great faith, Abram received a covenant blessing from God and was made the "Father of many nations", and God changed his name from Abram to Abraham (Genesis 12).

Prophecy was fulfilled when Jesus arrived on the scene. Remember, He was the only begotten son of God. Jesus was a descendant of Shem and a son of David, who was the son of Abraham. Jesus' inborn seed was placed in Mary's womb by the Holy Spirit. Jesus was chosen as the sacrificial "Lamb of God" to save the people from their sin (Matthew 1:21). Jesus paid the price and gave His life by an atonement made between God and man in order to redeem us from our sin. Jesus was recognized by His sacrifice of death, burial, and resurrection. He became the greatest leader of them all, and was truly an effective leader.

"So all this was done that it might be fulfilled which was spoken by the Lord through the prophet, saying: Behold, the virgin shall be with child, and bear a Son, and they shall call His name Immanuel," which is translated, "God with us" (Mat. 1:22-23)

In spite of the disassociation, disagreements, unbelief, and controversy between Jews and the Gentiles (non-Jews); now being in the Dispensation of Grace, not because God wants to show His love for all mankind and provide a way of deliverance for all people in the world; nor because they are his descendants are they all Abraham's children. On the contrary, it is through Isaac that your offspring will be reckoned.

In other words, "it is not the children by physical descent who are God's children, but it is the children of the promise who are regarded as Abraham's offspring" (Romans 9:7-8)

"For ye are all the children of God by faith in Christ Jesus" (Gal. 3:26)

"Even so we, when we were children, were in bondage under the elements of the world: But when the fullness of the time was come God sent forth His Son, made of a woman, made under the law, to redeem them that were under the law; that we might receive the adoption of sons. And because ye are sons, God hath sent forth the Spirit of His Son into our hearts, crying, Abba, Father" (Gal. 4:3-6)

"Know ye therefore know that only those who are of faith are sons of Abraham. And the scripture, foreseeing that God would justify the Gentiles by faith, preached the gospel to Abraham beforehand, saying, "In you all the nations shall be blessed. So then those who are of faith are blessed with believing Abraham" (Gal. 3:7-9)

Are you a believer? Now, do you know who you are? After looking at our ancestors in the Bible, I ask you, "Do you know about any leaders in your family? In the Bible, it seemed to be important for God to list the generations before us. It not only informs us of our ancestors, but it helps us know who the leaders were and how they served God.

When God gave Abraham the covenant of blessings and eternal life, He included all the generations (Acts 3:25-26), which includes us. Truly, these are our ancestors!

It is also important to know your family history in order to understand who you are. Learning who the leaders are in our families, gives forethought to the claim I made about our inborn leadership traits and abilities, as it appears throughout all generations.

Leadership and relationship in my family

In 1951, I was born in Omaha, Nebraska, located in the mid-western part of America. At that time, there were at least four generations of my family living. We presently continue to have close family ties and still enjoy having family reunions.

Many members of my family were scattered throughout the states. I am from a mixed (more than two) class of people from both my mother and father's side. There were many leaders in my family who loved God.

They made sacrifices to serve in the ministry of helping others.

I learned about my family's history by my ancestors, family historians, census and draft records, and from online genealogy websites which do not go back as far as I could've hope.

The limited information we received from others is why I believe it is also important to include the Bible as an additional resource. According to Schenck (2009), "The Bible is not some third path to truth – it is our first source of truth." It gives the history of our genealogy, and it shows when and where we originated. It also sets the precedent of knowing who we are today. It teaches us about our relationship with God.

I am the second born of four children. Presently, I have one sister, LaDonna (born in 1950); my only brother, Mark (1956-2014); and my younger sister, Satoya (born in 1960).

I remember riding the train to Cleveland, Ohio from Omaha, Nebraska, when I was three years old. Not long after we arrived in

Cleveland, that my alcoholic father left us after he and my mother found themselves in a heated and abusive argument. Not only was there broken glass everywhere, but this became a broken relationship between my mother and father. My sister and I were a witness to this abusive relationship. Every time the situation would occur, my sister would be prompted to sit in the hallway outside of our one-room apartment the four of us shared.

It seemed as though we were always sitting out in the hallway. This time it was different. It was the last time we would be sent to the hallway. It was the day our father left. Their relationship was finally over.

It can really be tough on everyone when your father does not accept his responsibility to take care of the family. I saw the suffering and pain in my mother's eyes, as she had to decide how she was going to raise two children on her own. I did not know what it meant to be abused. It was the first time I ever witnessed it. I eventually learned what it meant to survive. I can remember sharing one slice of bread for dinner between the three of us.

In those days, children were not allowed in different housing arrangements; so ultimately, we had to move.

As a child, I had to learn to adapt to many situations. Not knowing where we would end up living was one of them.

When relationships are broken, they either remain severed or become mended. There may be dim and bleak situations and circumstances we encounter in life, where we may not know what is going to happen next. One thing is for sure, God knows! Thankfully, we can depend on Him to be our Father and Leader who will watch over us.

My mother took the lead and went into a survival mode. In leadership, some would say this is a "situational leadership style". My mother had to take the lead according to the situation we were in. She had no book to follow. She had to find solutions to the problems we encountered after my father left. I believe this situation was predestined for us to experience – but why?

Could it be that God was revealing Himself by putting us in this situation in order for us to learn more about Him?

My sister and I ended up living with a lady called Ms. Newby while my mother managed to find work. I will never forget those days because it was during the time I was burned in a fire I started. I stuck my candied windmill in the fireplace to look at the beautiful colors blowing in the flames. I had no idea the fire was going to burn up my windmill or me. Once the fire got to the point of my fingers, I dropped it and began to feel pain as it started to burn my pants and leg.

I was truly "tried by the fire!" It was a different kind of pain compare to the sorrowful pain I felt as I looked into my mother's eyes after my father left. I did not know what I felt was also called pain, but I did know it hurt.

Could these feelings of pain and hurt have come from awareness or sensitivity that

God had thrust into my life to learn?

Was this a time I learn the difference in my emotions and the emotions of others? Ms. Newby was in a panic. My sister, on the other hand, did not seem to have any emotional response. She remained silent with anticipation of what was going to happen next. My mother seemed upset. She did not share her conversation with us after she spoke to Ms. Newby.

When people establish relationships they begin to trust and become responsible for each other. It was a good thing Ms. Newby did not take too long when she needed to go to the store to pick up something for lunch. The store was only a couple houses up the street.

When the pastor of Ms. Newby's church wanted to stop and talk to her, she truthfully admitted she had to hurry back, because we were home alone. Upon arriving back home, she heard me crying and screaming.

She then dropped the groceries and immediately ran upstairs to the parlor where she found me on fire. As she rolled me up in the rug and took me to the hospital, the doctor reported I had incurred 2nd and 3rd degree burns on my leg.

Whenever we are placed in a leadership role, we must understand the importance of making wise decisions. Our decisions can affect the lives of others. I am grateful because I may not be here today. It could have been another story to write about. Neither my sister nor I should have been left home alone, sitting in front of a fireplace.

Even at the age of three, I was concerned with what was going to happen next, and became fearful. Was my mother going to be angry and take us away from Ms. Newby? Or would she be mad at me, because of what I did; and not come back to visit us again? I often looked forward to seeing my mother on Saturdays when she would visit, even though there were times when those days became less frequent.

However, I learned to endure and enjoy whatever times we did have together, and not dwell on the bad times when she would not show up.

I believe through many situations we encounter in life, God is training us to become leaders. He teaches us to be patient, endurance, and to be more tolerant of others.

Shortly thereafter, my mother's friend offered us a place to stay. We were finally able to live together once again. It was a sigh of relief. Not long after, I began having dreams. One night, I had a dream about "Jesus" coming down from the ceiling. I was only four years old. I remembered seeing His picture from the Bible at the church Ms. Newby attended and would take us. I recognized Him and His robe.

He summoned my sister to follow Him. Yes, I was afraid. I ran and hid in my bedroom. I got down in the darkest corner to look through a peephole behind my bed and watched them go down the steps towards the door. At that very moment, He turned around and looked me right in my eye and told me, "Don't be afraid, I will be back for you". It is hard to explain, but it was something in His eyes that felt comforting, so I believed Him with much anticipation.

What was the purpose in this dream (vision)? Since that time, I have continued to wait for His return. I never had a dream like that again. During that time, I often wondered why He said He would come back for me. Who was I to Him that He would want to come back for me?

"Let integrity and uprightness preserve me; for I wait on thee" (Ps. 25:21)

"Leaders who display inspirational motivation and engagement to others provide meaningful and challenging work"

CHAPTER TWO

LEADERSHIP AND DISCIPLESHIP

Is leadership predestined by God?

Do you believe our identity and purpose is ordained in God?

"In the beginning, God created the heaven and the earth" (Gen. 1:1)

The scriptures reveal that the beginning of our identity is portrayed when God "made man in His image and likeness."

Once He was finished, God called all that He created "good" (Genesis 1:19-2:25). He was satisfied with His creation as it fulfilled His desire. Thus, we are "fearfully and wonderfully made" (Psalm 139:14). God desired an everlasting, righteous, loving relationship with man to create a sense of trust through faith, to be responsible to God and to one another. It has always been God's desire to reveal Himself in us since the time of creation (Romans 1:1-20). How's your relationship with God?

Throughout my life, God has shown me several leadership roles. Effective leadership is someone who is operational, current, sees the value in the people they lead, who work towards their vision, successfully reaches their goal while maximizing their potential. I consider this type of leadership as a servant leader within the body of Christ. This type of leader is closely defined as that of the transformational leadership style, which is a contemporary leadership model that enables followers to rise to a higher level of performance.

It is where both leaders and followers take each other to a higher level of growth through motivation and encouragement. It is the style in which I believe effective leadership is developed. According to transformational leadership theory, leadership does not reside in only an individual's thoughts, but in the relationship between individuals.

According to Bass (1990), "Leadership should be oriented to promote a vision, rather than focused solely on attaining organizational goals." Transformational leadership focuses on changing the human condition. It will empower individuals, at all organizational levels to assume leadership roles. Bass also indicates how transformational leaders inspire employees to exceed the expected by embracing a vision and striving to achieve that vision. "Transformational leaders demonstrate specific behaviors and actions through attributed charisma, inspirational motivation, intellectual stimulation, and individualized considerations" (Conger, 1999).

Attributed charisma occurs when leaders demonstrate behaviors that engender respect and trust. Leaders who display charisma and demonstrate an interest in the well-being of others, knows how to stay calm in crisis situations, formulate decisions that benefit the group as a whole, and demonstrate competence, will earn the respect of followers (Bass & Avolio, 1994).

Leaders who display inspirational motivation and engagement to others provide meaningful and challenging work. Intellectual stimulation includes not only creating dialogue, but promoting risk-taking and creativity by encouraging followers to question assumptions, redefine problems, and consider alternatives to existing methods or approaches. Individual consideration includes developing individualized relationships with followers to empower and support them.

Transformational leadership behaviors also increase followers' commitment to supporting the leader's vision, create innovative approaches, assume greater responsibility, and perform more effectively (Bass, 1990).

It is my belief those who envelop the transformational leadership style develop into effective leaders who may transform into discipleship.

The other main leadership styles include:

◊ *Autocratic style of leadership* - *Authoritarian leader who has control over all decisions and choices without any input from others.*

◊ *Democratic style of leadership – One who invites more input from others in decision making. Transactional style of leadership – A leader who is more focused on the bottom line profits and performance*

◊ *Situational/contingency style of leadership – Can adjust to the situation or what is the best fit to control and have influence over the outcome.*

◊ *Laissez faire style of leadership* – *Has no action in leading the group and delegates the group to make choices or handle the group or each other.*

What type of leader are you? I consider myself to be a transformational style leader.

Leadership thought and practice

According to the University of Phoenix material (2013), "leadership practice and philosophical study have occurred for centuries. The historical study of leadership requires examination of the significant periods and milestones of leadership thought from ancient times to the present." There are various theories and models of leadership. Leadership research is very important. It allows us to critique the way we lead and practice it.

The following historical information supports the high level of interest in and importance of leadership research. According to Wren (1995), during the 1500s Machiavelli reportedly commented that there were over

1,000 leadership books for sale; Bass (1990) reviewed over 3,000, pre-1974 leadership publications alone; and in the 21st century over 10,000 leadership references were available.

The Great Man Theory of the 19th Century and before, advocated that leaders were born rather than made, and that divine class or providence signified leadership. Plato's notion that leaders possessed inborn traits is echoed in much of the 20th-century literature prior to the middle of the 20th century. The Great Man Theory is what predominated leadership thought.

Consensus during this time was that leaders differed significantly from their followers. Bass (1990) explained that every society identified individuals who were intellectually and morally superior. These individuals were destined to lead. Proponents of the Great Man Theory suggest John F. Kennedy, Lee Iacocca, Douglas MacArthur, and Martin Luther King, Jr. are examples of individuals with inborn, predetermined leadership abilities.

As the behavioral sciences evolved, many would say the Great Man Theory has become less prevalent and more contemporary leadership models have emerged (Wren 1995).

As you can see, there are many books on contemporary leadership. The recipe for becoming an effective leader for Christ, and learning about discipleship, is not as available.

The lack of leadership at home, in the church, businesses, and other organizations brings the question of why many people find themselves making wrong decisions in life. Ultimately, not taking the time to learn what it takes to be an effective leader can cause people to be unsuccessful, possibly give up, and may even hinder the people they lead.

What is Discipleship?

Discipleship is the teaching of biblical precepts, while modeling and guiding others toward living righteously as followers of Jesus Christ. One of the most important characteristics of being a disciple is having an intimate relationship with God through Christ, rather than just learning about Him.

Discipleship equips Christians with God's Word, prayer, sound doctrine, worship, encouragement, service, develope goals, and moving in the assignment and purpose God has given.

Discipleship is based on what we believe God wants, not what we think we can do. "And Jesus came and spake unto them, saying, All power is given unto me in heaven and in earth. Go ye therefore, and teach all nations, baptizing them in the name of the Father, and of the Son, and of the Holy Ghost: Teaching them to observe all things whatsoever I have commanded you: and, lo, I am with you always, even unto the end of the world. Amen" (Matthew 28:18-20).

God uses people who want to help the church grow. Great leaders are just ordinary people who have an extraordinary amount of determination and stamina. "And let us not be weary in well doing for in due season we shall reap, if we faint not (Galatians 6:9).

You are never a failure until you quit. It is always too soon to give up.

"Though a righteous man falls seven times, he rises again" (Prov. 24:16)

Discipleship training takes commitment, vision, and understanding of the scriptures. In reading the words of Jesus (Matthew 28:18-20 NIV), we see that discipleship is not just an option for believers, but to the unbelievers.

"Then Jesus came to them and said, 'All authority in heaven and on earth has been given to me. Therefore go and make disciples of all nations, baptizing them in the name of the Father and of the Son and of the Holy Spirit, and teaching them to obey everything I have commanded you. And surely I am with you always to the very end of the age."

This is the commission to the Church.

"I began to learn to shift my mind, and to have faith in God for our deliverance"

Chapter Three

CHANGE YOUR MINDSET

Who are you?

God wanted me to change my mindset and heart to properly heal. I had witnessed a lifetime of turbulence and began to feel the inequality of life happening all around me. I had no idea what lessons the plans God had for me to learn in order to operate in high places and elevate in spiritual growth. God takes us through experiences to show how we must be aware of ways the enemy will try to weaken our minds through circumstances and distractions, to deter us from knowing who we are, and to keep us from becoming the believers and leaders we are called to be. We have to stay focused and encouraged.

Don't give up

I found that to be true in the schools I was attending. In elementary school I witnessed racial discrimination. This school had with a ratio of 30 Blacks to over 3,000 Caucasians. It was a requirement that no more than 2 black people could be in a classroom at a time. Whenever I got an "A" on my test, I was told I must have cheated and would have to take the test over. Of course, I would "ace" the test again, but I never got an apology. I was also a witness of age discrimination. I was an A/B student. I was told I could not graduate because I was too young (11 years old). I had to work in the office for (1) year, before I would graduate.

Unfortunately, I had no support from my family. No one stepped in on my behalf. I was told not to worry and that things would

Changing Your Mindset

get better. I guess they did not want to cause any problems with the school, since they had just moved to Garfield Heights, Ohio. I continued to encounter the bureaucratic practices between Garfield Heights and Cleveland school systems. During the time of graduating from High School, I was notified I would not graduate due to a miscalculation of a half-point in my credits. This news came after plans to start a new job, purchasing my pictures, robe and ring. I was told I had to take a class for a whole year before graduating. I had no one to advocate for me. I felt all hope for my future was lost. I gave up trying to make something out of my life and decided to dropped out of school. This is what happens when you depend on others, and not God! Where were the leaders who could have helped me get through this situation? Since I was still living at home, I was ordered to help my mother at our restaurant, if I was not going to go to school.

It was not long after, I was pregnant with my daughter. It was then when I realized this was not the life I wanted for me or my child.

My mother only paid me $25 a week. It certainly was not enough for us to live on. Most importantly, I believed I had a purpose and needed to pursue it. I needed to get my education to gain the knowledge necessary to reach my goals.

I was no longer going to let others keep me from progressing. It was done to our families hundreds of years ago during the days of slavery. I went back to school and graduated in spite of the fact that I encountered another set-back during graduation, in college.

This time, it was a little different. I received an apology and was asked to forgive them. Even though, I would never get those four years back that were taken away from me, I forgave them.

My point is, no matter what we go through know it does not mean we are to give up on life. We are to be determined to finish the task of our Divine assignment. God showed me how to take the lead, be responsible, to endure, be persistent, and be an overcomer. "I press toward the mark for the prize of the high calling of God in Christ Jesus" (Philippians 3:14). In addition, no matter how old you are it is never too late to get your education. Most importantly, do not let anyone keep you from getting your education. I was determined not to give my destiny away to the hands of the enemy. I managed to finally take the lead and complete my education. Now God is elevating me into assignments that will prepare me to be an effective leader.

God is in control

Many times we have a traditional understanding that causes us to see things differently, instead of what is obviously right in front of us. The reality for me was to know God is in control of my life. He had taken us from an environment of lack into an environment of prosperity.

When my mother re-married. We had a family. We ended up having a newly built home and a new car. My stepfather, Mark Sr., was a very informed and an intelligent business man. He owned a restaurant, a pool hall, and a few rental properties.

In the 50's, this was a major change of status. How important were all of these things if we didn't have God in our life? Where was all the love? Unfortunately, the more arguments and physical abuse happened between my parents, the more me and my siblings were also abused. If we were not beat with anything my mother would find, we were put under punishment for up to three months at a time.

I began to learn to shift my mind and to have faith in God for our deliverance. According to Romans 12:1-2, "I beseech you, therefore, brethren, by the mercies of God, that ye present your bodies a living sacrifice, holy, acceptable unto God, which is your reasonable service. And be not conformed to this world: but are ye transformed by the renewing of your mind, that ye may prove that which is good, acceptable, and a perfect will of God." God taught me how to have faith in Him and not in man.

I can truly attest to my faith in God. I began to make an increasingly radical change in my heart and my life. When I was younger, every summer, when my sister and I were seven and eight years old, my mother would put us on the Greyhound bus to go to Omaha, Nebraska where we would stay at either our grandmother's or our aunt and uncle's home. I can remember, at the age of 11, the day we arrived in Omaha, I lost sight in both my eyes. There was a blood clot in my left eye. I was two degrees from being permanently blind. My uncle rushed me to the hospital where I was admitted.

Each day the doctor continued removing the bandage from around my head. My family prayed that I would get my sight back. During that time, I remember God saying to me, "Everything will be all right." In my fearless thinking, I became grateful. God had at least given me a chance to see what everything looked like before going blind. I accepted what God told me and began to think about everything that had happened to me thus far.

Every day, I began thinking about where everything was situated before I left home so I would know my way around when I returned. I also envisioned the beautiful things God made, such as the flowers, the trees, the grass, the water, and the sky. As days went on, I continued thinking about how I needed to prepare my mind for whatever God had in store for me. It was at this point, I just didn't understand why this was happening to me, but I knew God was in control and "everything would be all right."

I could not think about school starting in a few weeks, or about my 12th birthday just around the corner. I kept thinking this must be what God wanted for me – to be blind. Maybe, this was something I would end up telling other people about and would share my story with others who were blind? Would I have to start learning how to read braille? I began to accept my condition. Every day God reassured me everything would be all right. I heard this before, I thought. I believed Him. This was an intimate time in my life where my spirit connected with God, and I was not afraid.

On the seventh day when the doctor took the bandages from my eyes, I alerted him that I could see blurry shadows of his hand. Then he asked how many fingers did I see? One, two, three...Oh my God! My vision became even clearer. I could then see my mom with tears in her eyes, my sister, my grandmother, and aunt and uncle standing around my bed, smiling with glee. "I can see! I can see!" I shouted with gladness.

Then my grandmother, a praying woman, said, "Thank you, Jesus! Our prayers were answered!" The emotions were high in the atmosphere as everyone began to thank God. Of course, I was happy and thanked God too! I guessed it just wasn't for me to be blind after all. I had the same thought during my burning experience. I learned God had more in store for me.

I wore a patch over my eye for the first three months after starting back to school. I didn't care about being laughed at or talked about because I knew God was watching over me. I am more than grateful He restored my sight.

As I noted, God is in control! Not only did this situation introduce the power of God and my faith in Him, but it showed me what it meant to be fully aligned with Him. He took full control of my life. When we fully submit to Him and are in alignment with Him, victory will come. This is my testimony: I am a child of God! I was blind, but now I see!

What's in your DNA?

According to The Genetics Home Reference (2013), "DNA (deoxyribonucleic acid) is the hereditary material in humans and almost all other organisms. It is often referred to as the building block of life. The arrangement of bases on the deoxyribose-phosphate backbone provides the codes necessary for life processes. Nearly every cell in a person's body has the same DNA. Most DNA is located in the cell nucleus (where it is called nuclear DNA). A small amount of DNA can also be found in the mitochondria (called mitochondrial DNA or mtDNA)."

Therefore, it is my thought that hereditary material is derived from the genetics of our ancestors.

The passing of these traits go from ancestor to descendant and is from a common stock deriving from a precursor (forerunner) or prototype of a true and effective leader (Christ Jesus). The Genetics Home Reference (2013) also states, "An important property of DNA is that it can replicate, or make copies of itself. Each strand of DNA in the double helix can serve as a pattern for duplicating the sequence of bases. This is critical when cells divide, because each new cell needs to have an exact copy of the DNA present in the old cell."

To sum it up, theoretically and genetically speaking, I understand that our DNA is the molecular basis of traits genetically derived from the passing of the original model (GOD). If we lose our identity (Christ Jesus) we lose our inheritance. God wants us to understand the value in what He has given us. That value is found in eternal life. "If ye know that He is righteous, ye know that every one that doeth righteousness is born of Him. And this is the record that God hath given to us in eternal life, and this life is in His Son. He that hath the Son hath life, and he that hath not the Son of God hath not life" (I John2:29; 5:11-14 and Amos 3:7).

It is my belief, the birth and justification through Jesus Christ (born of the seed, the root, the son of David; who is the son of Abraham, and the Son of God; the Holy One, both God and man, and the image of the invisible God as the Holy Spirit) gives credence as our link in knowing who we are by the acquisition of our heritage (Rom 1:3: 2 Tim 2:8; Rev. 22:16, Luke 1:35, John 10:30, Col 1:15).

Heritage, according to Webster's Dictionary, is a state of owning or a thing owned; our birthright, or position by which we are entitled by birth. Our inheritance is the birthright that gives us the possession and dominion God has promised us.

"For as many as are led by the Spirit of God, they are the sons of God. For ye have not received the spirit of bondage again to fear; but ye have received the Spirit of adoption, whereby we cry Abba, Father.

Changing Your Mindset

The Spirit itself beareth witness with our spirit, that we are the children of God: And if children, then heirs; heirs of God, and joint-heirs with Christ; if so be that we suffer with him, that we may be also glorified together"
(Rom. 8:14-17)

Today, if we understand who we are as leaders, have faith and believe God, His Covenant promise to us to receive eternal life, we will be able to use the power and authority we are given to overcome anything. Our growth as effective leaders will open many doors to many opportunities, enable us to move in God's will, and move in the plans He has in store for us in His kingdom. Yes, I knew there were others who went through things far worse than me. Although, many times I didn't think I had enough strength in me to sustain myself. I realized I couldn't do it alone. It was time for a real shift in my way of thinking.

The definition of shift means to exchange for, or replaced by another; and to change the place, position, or direction.

There is a shift in the poles on the planet, in the population of the world, and even a paradigm shift in what our position (or perspective) is in the Word of God. We have to see things differently. Let's take a closer look into our DNA.

"...experiences have taught me the importance of prayer, communication and love."

CHAPTER FOUR

JUSTIFICATION AND RECONCILIATION

We are justified by Christ

Justification is a legal term in which righteousness is imputed or credited to the person, rather to the change in him. By being justified by His grace, we are heirs according to the hope of eternal life. According to the Roget's' Thesaurus, the word justify, means to prove to be right, just, or reasonable; to exonerate, vindicate, acquit, absolve, pronounce free from guilt, blame, or to give one his due.

As stated above in Genesis 2, human unrighteousness caused separation from God. This action barred men and women from their fellowship and relationship with God. The wages of sin is the death which separated us from God. Separation from God is the beginning of death. Therefore, spiritual darkness and death were upon man and his descendants.

God had given dominion over His creation. But, broken fellowship destroyed the balance, purpose, and the righteous goal God had planned for mankind. "For whom he did foreknow, he also did predestinate to be conformed to the image of His Son, that he might be the firstborn among many brethren. Moreover whom he did predestinate, them he also called: and whom he called, them he also justified: and whom he justified, them he also glorified" (Romans 8:29-30).

By the sin of the first man's disobedience [Adam], all human beings became destined to become sinners, and death passed freely from one generation to another. (Phil. 2:8)

Justification & Reconciliation

> **To clarify, we are justified**

"by the coming of the second man [Jesus] who came to reverse the curse of sin on humanity by the grace of God, it was by obedience unto death all the way to the cross that we are saved" (Rom. 5:16-19)

Therefore, being justified by faith in Jesus Christ and by the grace of God we can rejoice in the hope of glory in the Kingdom of God. Ultimately, we are assigned to move in our purpose according to God's will (Romans 5:1-20). Ye see then how that by works a man is justified, and not by faith only (James 2:24). So, what is your purpose? What is your calling?

The word call, according to the Webster's Dictionary, is a means to announce authoritatively, as to summons, to make a request or demand, as to halt because of unsuitable conditions, to choose, appoint, elect, name, designate, and to demand surrender of, for redemption (a bond). Romans 5:18, describes justification of life as "God's way of securing an individual's righteousness and faith in His redemptive sacrifice through Jesus Christ, to be given to all men."

We cannot be counted to be just by God and live in sin at the same time. The body cannot be both dead and alive at the same time. This is why God provided a way of atonement and restoration. By the Sacrificial Lamb of God on the cross, God's justification led to sanctification and His righteousness reigns in us all. It is the faith which changes our position with God and brings a radical change in our hearts and lives.

What is reconciliation?

God, who through Christ, reconciled us to Himself and gave us the ministry of reconciliation. Whatever we find ourselves going through in life, there is no other way around it. You cannot handle your circumstances alone!

God wants to have a relationship with mankind and wants to heal the land.

Justification & Reconciliation

Reconciliation is the restoration of a friendly relationship between two or more parties. It is the reuniting, reunion, bringing together (again), reconcilement, and agreement.

"If my people, which are called by my name, shall humble themselves, and pray, and seek my face, and turn from their wicked ways; then will I hear from heaven, and will forgive their sin, and will heal their land."
(II Chronicle 7:14)

The world can be healed through reconciliation with God if they would seek Him and turn away from their sinful ways. He is our provider. We can also pray with the expectation of miracles by asking God to bring deliverance and healing by using our God-given power to heal the sick and raise the dead. In the time of need, God is our Way Maker. In the midst of a storm and our Doctor when we need a healer. We can go to Him and be victorious in whatever we are going through.

Reconciling my family relationships

When I was married to my children's father, I found myself in an abusive relationship three years after my son was born. It was something I was too familiar with. It would start with verbal and mental abuse. Then, it became physical abuse. I never expected it would ever happen to me, but I was wrong. I knew there was no love left for me if things ever got to that point. It was against my moral values to stay and continue to be abused. Physical abuse is an extremely dangerous situation, and someone has to get out of that situation before something drastic would happen. After witnessing my mother and father's abusive relationship, I knew there was no way I was going to stay and endure such pain and agony. I did not want my children to have to witness such practice.

No one should ever have to go through such trauma! We not only rob each other of the life God has in store for us, but we destroy our relationship when we become abusive towards each other. Although it only happened once, it was enough for me!

Justification & Reconciliation

No matter how many times I heard the words "I'm sorry", I had to stand on my morals. I always believed this type of relationship is not built on love, but is of the devil.

In spite of the fact that I didn't want to leave my home and because I knew it would be difficult to start our lives over, I had to take the risk and be responsible for the lives and safety of my children. I had to get away.

Not knowing exactly what I was going to do, I had to act on instinct. When my husband finally went to work, I had only a short amount of time to make a move. It was on a Friday. He was not planning to work on the weekend. I knew we had to get out of the house before this situation would get worse once he came home. Fortunately, with the help of God, we got away safely.

I was grateful for one of my girlfriends coming to our rescue and allowing us to stay with her. My nightly tears increased as I wailed in my disappointment. I began feeling like I had failed as a wife and as a mother.

It became a time when I felt everything was getting out of control. After growing up in that type of environment, which also took place between my mother and my stepfather, I promised myself I would never subject my children to have such a life. However, my struggles led to more problems. Eventually, the type of environment we were living in was not healthy. I could have ended up as an alcoholic, a drug addict, or even become suicidal. However, I did not want my children to live under those circumstances or feel the pain of losing me. After all, why would I have left my marriage if I was only going to end up in a more tragic state than I had just escaped from?

Although, there were more things that happened to me during our marriage, I cannot begin to express the pain and anguish I had to succumb to while trying to make our marriage work. Those were the times I kept many things to myself because others would have reacted differently on my behalf. At times my anger began to get the best of me and things could have led to others being hurt, or even eliminated.

Justification & Reconciliation

When it comes to broken relationships and family members are involved, we have to make the right decisions to protect everyone-- such as those who would want to come to our rescue or defense. This is why I could not get everyone involved in what I went through. They could have ended up paying for their actions the rest of their life. Our children and families could have suffered a much greater loss. However, we must learn to go to God to make right decisions and see the bigger picture for us to have the best outcome for everyone-- even if it meant I would be the one getting hurt and ending up suffering alone.

Such events ultimately took away my trust in everyone. I needed to protect my children from them. It was a time for me to get a grip of myself and take the lead. I knew it was more important to protect them from suffering the way I suffered. As time went on, I had so much anger stored in me I needed to repent of my ways. I prayed more to God than ever before. I had so much hatred for people it felt like my heart was wrapped with wire. I tried to shut everyone out of my life, except for my children.

Thankfully, God never gave up on me. He continued to show His love, and He saved me from the depression and the disappointment in myself. Eventually, I asked God to forgive me and to help me regain my love for others.

God taught me a new way of life. First, He showed me I needed to forgive myself and then to forgive others. When my children's father asked me to forgive him for what he had done and all the pain and suffering he had caused me, surprisingly I forgave him and asked him to forgive me as well. You see, being in a relationship is a two-way street. No matter what happened, I managed to turn my feelings back towards a love for him. Thankfully, we continue to be on good terms. I recognized how reconciliation is a benefit to all people. Rather than to let things turn into situations we may regret. We can gain an opportunity to move forward in our lives.

At the age of 33, I joined my church and gave much of my time towards the ministry. I was in attendance almost every day of the week. Many relationships developed there.

Justification & Reconciliation

The members of my church ultimately became my extended family. I thought this would be a foundation we definitely needed. However, there seemed to be turmoil between some of the members. Sin and discord were slowly creeping in. There were disagreements, jealousy, and even fights between the families.

I thought Christianity was never meant to be dictated, but it was meant to be demonstrated. However, I did not see the love, encouragement, empowerment, or much spiritual development according to our gifts, or talents, being manifested or present there. We were not given any real direction or encouragement, or spiritual growth to become leaders for Christ in the Kingdom of God. The directions there consisted more about staying away from sin and not going to hell.

As a single parent, I realized I had to learn how to communicate and be more transparent with my children, and had to become a good role model. There were so many issues from my past.

I didn't know what it meant to be a good role model as a parent. I did not get the love I needed at home when I was growing up because we were busy surviving. I needed to learn how to find a balance between family, church, school, and work; but that was not easy!

Since I was not raised feeling a lot of love, I made a point to show my love for my children no matter how long it took. My children needed to understand God's love and the love I had for them. They needed to understand what it meant to have God in their lives as their father. It was because of God's love for us, and our faith in Him, that we remained hopeful that we would one day be all right. We eventually began to spend more time together, but it did not seem to be enough. There was still something missing.

On Easter Sunday, in 1984, I was saved and filled with the precious gift of the Holy Spirit. That was the love that filled the void in my life. I felt I was made complete. I was on top of the world and could conquer anything that came against me.

It was then when I began to pray and ask God to give all of my children a desire to be saved, and to help them learn more about Him. As time went on, God answered my prayers. Each of my children and grandchildren are saved. I count this as my greatest blessing, and count it all joy! Now they have become leaders in their family and in the community by helping others. They have learned to establish their relationship with God as well.

The above experiences have taught me the importance of prayer, communication, and love. These are some of the major keys in life and being a leader. Communication develops relationships. It is a way to bring others together in Christ. As I shared, I was not raised where my parents showed much love, communication, or were encouraging to us. My siblings and I grew up in an unfavorable and strict environment where there was a lot of negativity spoken into our lives. The Word of God says,

"Let no corrupt communication proceed out of your mouth, but that which is good to the use of edifying, that it may minister grace unto the hearers" (Eph. 4:29)

No matter where you are as a leader, you must communicate and share some love to the people you lead.

"The Kingdom is based on the principals of Love"

CHAPTER FIVE

ARE YOU CONNECTED TO GOD?

The power of prayer

As a Christian, it is important to communicate with God. You can do this through prayer. Prayer changes things. I would pray for God to deliver me and release me from the strongholds that kept me in bondage. Through all of your trials and tribulations, you might believe you have experienced everything in life. Although that was not true, it just feels like it. God only gives us what we can handle.

Ultimately, when we pray we must be persistent and not pray aimlessly. As leaders, we are to walk and pray in the spirit. It is by the power of prayer we find our supernatural walk. Prayer is our spiritual portal to God.

"And pray in the Spirit on all occasions with all kinds of prayers and requests. With this in mind, be alert and always keep praying for all the Lord's people" (Eph. 6:18 NIV)

Since we are no longer bound in the Mosaic Laws and now are living in the Dispensation of Grace (Ephesians 3:1-21), we have an opportunity to go directly to God through prayer. I am more than grateful for the door God opened for us to communicate directly to Him because of the death, burial, and resurrection of Jesus Christ. As leaders, God gives us the instructions to prepare for what is to come when we pray.

By faith and prayer we form our relationship with God, and are transformed into direct communication with Him by the quickening of the Holy Spirit.

Ultimately, I believe prayer is the door that will introduce us to our God-given purpose. That purpose is to become an effective leader, as were the Disciples of Christ, to save souls. "Brethren, my heart's desire and prayer to God for Israel is that they might be saved" (Romans 10:1).

As a Disciple of Christ, being an effective leader will broaden the stakes of our tents to become more dedicated to God, while equipping others. The stakes of our tents are broadened by the intercessors who will express the love and vision God has for us and others.

When we pray, we must acknowledge God for the great God He is and give Him the glory and the honor in all that He has done, and is doing in our lives. It is necessary that leaders come boldly to the throne of grace and to pray boldly in the Spirit. When we intercede in the intercessory prayer for others with a faith message of deliverance, our prayers can ultimately lead the nations back to God.

Faith in God

It is written,

"Now faith is the substance of things toped for, the evidence of things not seen"
(Hebrews 11:1)

Through faith, believers understand the world was framed by the Word of God. Some leaders, such as Enoch and Noah who became heirs of righteousness, had faith to trust in God in saving others.

Abraham received an inheritance because he had faith in God. And his heirs, Isaac and Jacob, also received the same promise. Through faith, Sara and Abraham received strength to conceive a seed when they were past age. By faith, Moses forsook Egypt by choosing to suffer in affliction with the people of God, as they passed through the Red sea where the Egyptians were drowned. David, Samuel, and the prophets also need faith to make it through the tribulation period, in order to become effective leaders in the Kingdom of God.

We must have faith in God, that one day we will have no more pain or suffering, and will have everlasting life. It is also the power of our prayers and faith that keep some leaders from giving up. I believe we are called by God for such a time as this.

"And, we know all things work together for good of them that love God, to them who are called according to his purpose"
(Rom. 8:28)

Although there were times I wavered in my faith, I refused to give up. I knew God had begun a work in me and would bring it to completion (Philippians 1:6). He has the same plan for others.

"Behold, I will do a new thing; now it shall spring forth; shall ye not know it? I will even make a way in the wilderness, and rivers in the desert."
(Isaiah 43:19)

"Being aligned with God gives us an opportunity to be prepared for change, and to allow new ideas to come"

CHAPTER SIX

ARE YOU SPIRITUALLY ALIGNED WITH GOD?

What is alignment?

According to Webster's Dictionary, alignment is the state of being aligned; in proper positioning or state of adjustment. Are you willing to put God's preference above your own? The thought of being aligned and pleasing to God should be important to you. There should be an inside compassion to please God, to do His will, be transformed, and renewed by Him.

In spite of the structured methods, different interpretations of the scriptures, commentaries, narratives on the context of Biblical text; as sons of God, we can look to the scriptures to learn how to become leaders and live our daily lives. In reading the scriptures, we learn how to discern God's Word through the guidance of the Holy Spirit. It is then when we can recognize His voice and His will, and become spiritually aligned to Him.

It is also important to have faith in God's Word and not in the traditions and interpretation of men. In Paul's letters for example, there are some things that are hard to understand, which some people tend to distort. This is the error of lawlessness, by those who do not have a firm foundation of God or the Spirit of God. There is no confusion in God or in His Word.

Scripture tells us how we must repent of our ways, guard our minds, have faith, trust and believe, and be aligned with God.

Are You Spiritually Aligned?

"Examine yourselves, whether ye be in the faith; prove your own selves. Know ye not your own selves, how that Jesus Christ is in you, except ye be reprobates" (II Cor. 13:5)

Alignment in God comes when we clear our mind from our old ways and move into a new ways of thinking. It is a matter of becoming new. t states,

"If any man is in Christ he is a new creature (creation): old things are passed away: behold all things have become new."

We must get away from the old way of thinking, speaking, and acting. Being aligned with God gives us an opportunity to be prepared for change and to allow new ideas to come. When we are aligned with God, we are equipped and prepared to be the Disciples of Christ and we must understand this walk will not be easy.

"Finally, my brethren, be strong in the Lord, and in the power of his might. Put on the whole armour of God, that ye may be able to stand against the wiles of the devil.

For we wrestle not against flesh and blood, but against principalities, against powers, against the rulers of the darkness of this world, against spiritual wickedness in high places" (Eph. 6:10-12)

There are many people who will come against you, and you will have to contend or deal with them during your transformation period.

Additionally, if we are to cast out any wrong spirits, we must be sure we are properly aligned with God, learn to repent, and confess our sin. Do you have a clean heart? As a leader, does the enemy have a claim on you due to unconfessed sin? There is sweetness over victory, if there is repentance. We must get in alignment and find our balance with the business of God, as Peter did after he repented.

Power and authority

Through prayer and provision, God continues to show His love for mankind by appointing leaders of His governmental office.

"And he gave some, apostles; and some, prophets; and some, evangelists; and some, pastors and teachers; For the perfecting of the saints, for the work of the ministry, for the edifying of the body of Christ: Till we all come in the unity of the faith, and of the knowledge of the Son of God, unto a perfect man, unto the measure of the stature of the fullness of Christ: to train, and equip the saints for spiritual growth, for the work of the ministry"
(Eph. 4:11-13)

The authority of our divine assignment does not come from others. Romans 13:1-5 states,

"Let every soul be subject unto the higher powers. For there is no power but of God: the powers that be are ordained of God. Whosoever therefore resisteth the power, resisteth the ordinance of God: and they that resist shall receive to themselves damnation. For rulers are not a terror to good works, but to the evil. Wilt thou then not be afraid of the power? do that which is good, and thou shalt have praise of the same:

For he is the minister of God to thee for good. But if thou do that which is evil, be afraid; for he beareth not the sword in vain: for he is the minister of God, a revenger to execute wrath upon him that doeth evil. Wherefore ye must needs be subject, not only for wrath, but also for conscience sake."

It is not up to man to reject the mandate or authority God has placed on you. It is up to God to give and remove authority from people in the spiritual and secular environment. In God's mandate to the church, He gives us the power and authority as the Sons of God to be led by the Holy Spirit, as we are appointed to be Disciples to preach and teach the Gospel of Christ (Romans 8:14)

At times, we find ourselves in circumstances of life that keep us controlled by systems that keep us bound and we fail to realize we have been given power to break free. God gave us the authority and power to complete the assignment He has given us. We must recognize the principles of His authority and power. The Kingdom is based on the principals of Love; and good must overcome evil (Luke 4:36, NKJV). Our power comes from the Holy Spirit within and not from without. If we have faith and believe that we are protected by the hand of God in everything we go through, we will have the power to overcome. When we go through a storm, things may not make sense. God has dealt with every man according to a measure of faith. He gives us strength and power to make the journey. Although there are times we long for happiness and celebrating with our loved ones, God says,

"but seek ye first the kingdom of God and His righteousness, and all these things will be given unto you" (Matt. 6:33)

It is when we are not in compliance with what God wants from us, we tend to miss out on the things God has in store for us. Thus, we run the risk of missing critical assignments, kingdom connections, and we lose focus. As leaders, having kingdom connections gives us hope and something to look forward to. God has given authority to you to become an effective leader.

Divine deliverance

When we believe in God, we learn to trust that He will deliver us, while He is strengthening and preparing us for eternal life. God gives everyone the same opportunity to get to know Him.

> *"But God sent me ahead of you to preserve for you a remnant on earth and to save your lives by a great deliverance" (Gen. 45:7)*

Divine deliverance is given to those who follow Christ.

> *"For I know that through your prayers and God's provision of the Spirit of Jesus Christ what has happened to me will turn out for my deliverance. (Phi. 1:19 NIV)*

Unfortunately, there are still others who do not know who God is, and they are the souls that need to be saved. There is much work for us to do before this world comes to an end. Jesus is the only way, the only truth and the only light in this dark world. We must have faith that deliverance will come (II Cor. 5:20).

We must believe the Lord's promise to release us. It is time to be released to walk in spiritual authority and spiritual excellence.

"Thou art my hiding place; thou shalt preserve me from trouble; thou shalt compass me about with songs of deliverance" (Ps. 32:7)

If we remember Jesus is in the midst of our storms, we can stay focused on the promise and not the problem.

"Nay, in all these things we are more than conquerors through him that loved us." (Rom. 8:37)

*And it shall come to pass, that whosoever shall call on the name of the L<small>ORD</small> shall be delivered.
(Joel 2:32a)*

"For I know that through your prayers and God's provision of the Spirit of Jesus Christ what has happened to me will turn out for my deliverance" (Phil. 1:19 NIV)

Finding my balance

Nine years after my divorce from my abusive relationship, God brought someone into my life. He was someone who put God first and loved me and my family. We were married for 10 years. My kids were happy for me because they saw a real change in our environment. We had peaceful and happy times. We were as a whole family again. We enjoyed each other, the lines of communication were open with one another, took family trips, had celebrations, and special times together. I felt our lives were on track. I truly believe God delights in making up for what we lack. We are meant to depend on Him to make provision for us, as He supplies all of our needs. He said, "He will never leave us nor forsake us" (Mat 6:25-34)

As parents, we try to keep our children on the paths we want for them. However, when they reach maturity and no longer want to rely on our direction, it becomes difficult for us to release them into the world, without worrying. Yet, we have to learn to let them go, so they can become more responsible and independent. When it is time for your children to grow on their own, God will further develop them.

In the last three years of my marriage, my husband became very ill with heart and lung disease (COPD). It was a struggle for him and us to see his life diminish right before our eyes. Even the hospital could no longer help him. As we prepared for his transition, he asked to go to hospice. On the day after, on May 31, 2001, God released him from this world. Such a loss was the beginning of a real crisis in our family. I began to ask God what we were going to do and prayed God would give me strength.

The after effects of my loss increased. Four months later, my son went to prison in Mississippi (of all places) and was sentenced to eight years. I found myself trying to succumb to surviving and keeping my sanity. This situation was definitely out of my control. I remember praying and asking God to "take the wheel". Is this what it takes when we pray for more strength? I could not mourn my husband's death or my son's absence, because I certainly felt I had no strength left.

I knew the next eight years was going to be hard for me to handle. I was so upset with everything that had happened and became distraught and unsatisfied with myself.

I began to think God had given up on me when my prayers seem to have gone unanswered. I felt there was no way I could handle anything. I began to feel worthless and wanted to give up after falling into a backslidden state of disrepair.

This was a time I experienced a real "roller coaster ride" in my life. It was a time when God had to step in to show me He had something even greater for me. What was I going to experience next?

When I look back over all that I had gone through, I thought I had gone through enough. Unfortunately, that was not true. I began to encounter a multitude of situations. There were illnesses and deaths in my family that required my attention. I was told my mother had fourth stage ovarian cancer and had maybe two years left to live. At the same time, my niece needed a third transplant; but she died within the month when she caught pneumonia in the hospital.

It was at this time, I felt I was being pulled from all sides, and my mind was being overloaded.

Then God answered my prayers and sent help. At the time of preparing for my niece's funeral, my family came from Nebraska and Colorado to our rescue. The same thing happened when my mother passed. During the time of her funeral, my family and friends were there to help us out. I cannot explain how grateful I am to everyone for stepping in. God also sent some of my friends to actually put money in my hand, and gave me their vehicle to transport my family.

The sickness and death of my niece and my mother was more than I could handle, but I had to help my siblings get through it.

In the midst of these circumstances, I also had a confrontation with my tenant who refused to pay rent. Sometimes, when you try to help people during bad times in life, they will take advantage of your kindness and will add to your pain or suffering, because they have no concern for you, only themselves.

I found this to also be true in my church. There were many who were too busy asking me for help with their needs; they never thought to ask me how I was doing, or if I needed anything. I believe there were some who may have gotten mad at me for not attending their birthday parties, graduations, baby showers, sending Christmas gifts, or spending time with them. If it was possible where I had enough money, or time, I would try to show up and participate, but there was just too much going on in my life.

Are You Spiritually Aligned?

They may not have been aware of my struggles, because they eventually stopped calling me. Some people just cannot give you the love that God can give you.

There were some who tried to take away my humility, my integrity, and even my power while they stood around playing games on each other. Some would try to distract me from what God had in store from me. And some would also watch to see how far I would fall, so they would have something to talk about. Those were people who may not have had their own life to worry about.

"And the brother shall deliver up the brother to death, and the father the child: and the children shall rise up against their parents, and cause them to be put to death. And ye shall be hated of all men for my name's sake: but he that endureth to the end shall be saved" (Matthew 10:21-22).

After many stumbles I had to get a grip of myself to use the power, knowledge, and wisdom God gave me to be an overcomer.

God's plan for me was being developed, but during those times, I felt as if I was losing my mind. Did I feel helpless? Yes! Did I blame those who seemed to disregard what I was going through, and took advantage of my vulnerability? Yes! Did I stop praying or did I lose my faith in God? No! I refused to give up! I repented and prayed for forgiveness, for the anger I had felt towards God and His people.

I knew I had an uphill battle to climb and needed to recognize I was not in this alone. Even in my darkest hours, I had gained enough faith to know God was going to fight my battles and give me what I needed to get back on my feet. After all, how could I take care of others, if I could not take care of myself? God stepped in and rescued me from me, once again. I have learned my experiences are what adds to my spiritual growth and development in my relationship with Him.

"It is about kingdom trajectory."

CHAPTER SEVEN

PREPARING FOR DESTINY

Are you equipped and prepared?

Part of the process of being equipped includes:

- ◊ *Making God your priority through transformation and repentance (Mark 8:34-38)*

- ◊ *Learning and living by the written Word of God with commitment (John 8:31-32)*

- *Allowing God to direct us in loving, edifying, and serving others (1 John 3:11-16)*
- *Focusing on a fruitful and righteous living (John 15:7-10, Galatians 5:22)*

- *Being accountable for godly authority (Hebrews 13:17)*

Foundational values of discipleship:

- *Sharing the Gospel of Jesus Christ through Evangelism (Matthew 28:18-20)*

- *Renewing our minds and allowing for change (Romans 12:2)*

- *Always acknowledging and worshipping God (Romans 12:1)*

- *Moving in and operating in God's Word and the Holy Spirit (1 Corinthians 12:7-11; 2 Peter 1:3-8)*

◊ *Serving God in your purpose (Romans 1:9)*

Our actions to help others can be used by God's Spirit to bring them closer to Him. This provides the opportunity to introduce others to God's love and grace. We should never quit learning and growing in our walk with Christ. With all of the things I have gone through, it has been an ongoing process and a life-long experience. Just as the disciples who were chosen to follow Jesus and have a relationship with Him, they learned to grow stronger in their relationship with God through servitude.

Time is of the essence . We are in the last days. God says in Isaiah 1:19, "If ye be willing and obedient, ye shall eat the good of the land." So go and sin no more." As mentioned above, we must restore our relationship with God through repentance and alignment. Be persistence in developing our God-given purpose. We are to humble ourselves to God as well.

Humility is a vital part of the discipleship. All believers are to pursue with love and obedience. We must be obedient and move from just playing church to being the church. Peter tells us to be humble toward others so we can learn of the grace of God.

Finally, when we exhibit a joy-filled, love-filled heart with the excitement of a better life and promise of eternity with Christ in the Kingdom of God, we will want to share it with the world? According to the scripture,

"For God did not send His Son into the world to condemn the world, but to save the world through him" (John 3:17)

Are you ready to serve God? We are God's representatives and ambassadors, and we are responsible to carry out the orders of God according to Ephesians 4:11-16.

God gave us power and authority as leaders to empower, edify, replenish, renew, and equip others for the work of the ministry. It is a major part of our ministry based on the principals of love, and it encompasses how the good must overcome evil. It is our mandate that we acknowledge the gift of God, which is eternal life; and expound on the Word of God to teach the gospel and prepare others to serve Him.

Christians, who believe the Bible holds authority over them, take the task of application or appropriation, which is the final step in the process. "Knowing how to make the final jump from the text to life is the most critical skill of all, because it is the one that determines how the Bible can impact your life" Schenck (p. 8), "Our appropriations must adhere to the rule of faith, the consensus of the church as in regards to our belief, and must adhere to the royal "Law of love" (p. 84).

Our territory is within spiritual authority and is developed through our sphere of love. As the muscle in the arm of love is our measure of rule in leadership, we must lead by inspiration, and not by intimidation.

"Though I speak with the tongues of men and of angels, and have not charity, I am become as sounding brass, or a tinkling cymbal. And though I have the gift of prophecy, and understand all mysteries, and all knowledge; and though I have all faith, so that I could remove mountains, and have not charity, I am nothing. And though I bestow all my goods to feed the poor, and though I give my body to be burned, and have not charity, it profiteth me nothing" (1 Cor. 13:1-3)

God is not looking at our ability, but humility and love. Once you hear God's voice and become obedient to His Word, you will be able to speak whatever He wants you to say to others, and you will have learned to identify spiritual authority as you understand your divine assignment, as it is given (Romans 12:1). After all, it is your reasonable service.

A Disciple of Christ is not a self-given title or demand for respect, but is given on the basis of being Christ-like, being holy, as in His nature, His heart, His vision, and His purpose.

God calls us and assigns a spiritual ministry, as a confirming voice by the Holy Spirit, and as guidance to learn of the Kingdom of God by revealing His Word in our life.

God's spiritual authority will allow us to be bold and take a stand in the power we are given. It will enable us to become effective leaders who will have the opportunity to save other nations. It will give us boldness with love and truth – not exaggeration, not with hatred; but by the unction and anointing of the Holy Spirit and the Word of God. So let us ask for spiritual revival and a new mindset. Such anointing will come from the Spirit of God and others will be saved through our effectiveness.

It is my intent to emphasize the appropriation in God's Word and to prepare for the end times and the Kingdom of God. As mentioned above, our purpose is for God to be manifested in our lives and the lives of others, through His Word and from the Holy Spirit. It is the route or course we must take in preparing others to be effective leaders in the Kingdom of God, and is our focus on the process of God's strategic plan for developing and preparing spiritual and effective leaders.

We will discover a new way of living, by becoming Christ-like and having a new mindset in the way we serve Him and each other. In order to develop as effective leaders and to become as Disciples of Christ, and to be empowered and equipped to preach, teach, save, and equip others to be effective leaders in their community and in the world.

- CONCLUSION -

The grace of God has blessed my family. We are constantly growing in our endeavors to make a difference in the lives of others in schools, organizations, in the community, and around the world. If we take care of God's business, He will take care of us. Just because our route has been recalculated, our destiny has not changed. The power and authority given to us allows us to rise above the challenges of life. Ultimately, it is God's desire to be glorified and manifested in each of us.

We are the church, as members in one body – the Body of Christ. If we are born to be effective leaders, and if we trust God and honor His Word, and believe in His will, we can give the world everything they need to come to Christ. As mentioned earlier, if we lose our identity (Christ Jesus), we will lose our inheritance as heirs. We must understand who we are.

As effective leaders, we must live by the promise God has given us,

"The Lord is not slow in keeping his promise, as some understand slowness. Instead, He is patient with you, not wanting anyone to perish, but everyone to come to repentance." (II Peter 3:9 NIV)

The reason the Son of God appeared was to destroy the devil's work" (1 John 3:8).

"But in keeping with His promise we are looking forward to a new heaven and a new earth, where righteousness dwells"

(II Peter 3:13 NIV)

The Bible reveals the tribulation period and what is to come. Most importantly, God relays His vision for us to have eternal life. His seed is the Word of God. It is in scripture that God gives us an understanding of His purpose and vision for mankind, and we must trust God's Word for who we are. The Spirit of God brings transformation and we will be totally transformed in due time.

Through transformation, we must change our mindset, mend our relationship and fellowship with Him, and recognize all of the glory, praise, and honor in all we do, belongs to Him.

"Now all has been heard; here is the conclusion of the matter: Fear God and keep his Commandments, for this is the duty of all mankind" (Eccl.12:13)

We were predestined by God as born leaders. No matter how much or little education we may have, everything we need from God is already in us. Now is the time for us to be about our Father's business.

As leaders, God brings us together to learn from each other, and to work together to save and prepare others for that "open heaven". It is essential to stay focused on what God wants from us as we prepare for eternal life in His kingdom.

"Beloved, I wish above all things that thou mayest prosper and be in health, even as thy soul prospereth" (3 John 2)

It is then, when we can be a vessel for Christ and to abide in His presence.

"And that he might reconcile both unto God in one body by the cross, having slain the enmity thereby: And came and preached peace to you which were afar off, and to them that were nigh. [18] For through him we both have access by one Spirit unto the Father. Now therefore ye are no more strangers and foreigners, but fellow citizens with the saints, and of the household of God; And are built upon the foundation of the apostles and prophets, Jesus Christ himself being the chief corner stone; [21] In whom all the building fitly framed together groweth unto an holy temple in the Lord: [22] In whom ye also are built together for an habitation of God through the Spirit" (Eph. 2:16-22)

Our life and love for God should be inseparable.

Who shall separate us from the love of Christ? Shall tribulation, or distress, or persecution, or famine, or nakedness, or peril, or sword? As it is written, for thy sake we are killed all the day long; we are accounted as sheep for the slaughter. Nay, in all these things we are more than conquerors through him that loved us. For I am persuaded, that neither death, nor life, nor angels, nor principalities, nor powers, nor things present, nor things to come, nor height, nor depth, nor any other creature, shall be able to separate us from the love of God, which is in Christ Jesus our Lord" (Rom. 8:35-39)

    I pray you now understand what it means to be an effective leader, and you are ready to become a Disciple of Christ. Do you believe God for what He has done for us? I believe it is time to be about our Father's business!

I give all the honor and praise to God for His grace and mercy, for restoring our relationship with Him, for allowing us to stay connected, and for equipping us with the Word, and with a desire to serve Him with excellence, as a Disciple for Christ.

May the grace and peace of God be upon you! Be blessed!

Dr. Mattie Shaw

- ABOUT THE AUTHOR -

Dr. Mattie C. Shaw was born in Omaha, Nebraska, and has lived in Cleveland, Ohio, for over 60 years. Dr. Shaw is a mother of two, Nichole and Michael; and has two granddaughters, Brittani and Jazmyn. In 1994, she became a Spirit–Filled believer. She was ordained in 2015, as an Elder by Apostle Martin L. Griffin, Founder of Victory Temple International (VTI) and Equipping Ministries International (EMFI), in Cleveland, OH, and has contributed most of her life in the love of doing the work of the ministry and enjoys helping people who need assistance in sustainability in life.

"I believe it is my mission to give back to society by helping others in need".

Dr. Shaw believes education is vital to our existence. She has received a degree of Associate of Arts, a Bachelor of Science of Management, a Master of Art of Ministry/Leadership from Indiana Wesleyan University and Seminary in Marion, IN, and a Doctorate of Divinity, from Isaiah University in Orlando, FL.

"Without education you would not be able to read the Word of God or learn to read The Bible to get the truth."

While writing her book, Dr. Shaw took inventory of her leadership abilities and recognized the different levels of influence that impacted her--- while displaying episodes of her life, using her experiences as testimonies in her spiritual development. It is the revelation of discipleship that she realized her purpose as a leader and became founder of both her organization and company, Connectivity of Missions Empowerment and Beracah Solutions, LLC.

Presently Dr. Shaw seeks to develop her vision of managing areas of education and community outreach programs around the world.

Dr. Mattie C. Shaw is also an Advocate for Research in Disabilities and Accessibility, serving the Youth and the Elderly. Her services include:

> Speaker - Teacher – Mentor - Consultant

Outreach Programs/ Educational Seminars/ Workshops

◊ Leadership Training and Development

◊ Wellness and Empowerment Programs

◊ Social and Environmental Protection

Mattie C. Shaw, AA, BSM, MML, DD

Contact via email: mshaw7077@yahoo.com

Connectivity of Missions Empowerment (COME)

REFERENCES

All About Following Jesus (2002 – 2018) All AboutFollowingJesus.org, Retrieved from https://www.allaboutfollowingjesus.org/bible.htm?embed_path=/query&query=Romans%201:9.

Aristotle (n. d.). Politics. In T. J. Wren (Ed.), (1995). The Leaders Companion: *Insights on leadership through the ages.* Free Press. New York, N.Y. (p. 65).

Bass, B. M., & Avolio, B. J. (1994). Improving Organizational Effectiveness through Transformational, Leadership, Sage Publications. Thousand Oaks, CA.

Bass, B. M. (1990). Concepts of Leadership: *The beginnings.* In T. J. Wren (Ed.), (1995) The Leaders Companion: *Insights on leadership through the ages.* Free Press. New York, N.Y.

Bass, B. M. (1990). Bass & Stogdill's Handbook of Leadership: *Theory, research, & managerial applications* (*3*). Free Press. New York, NY.

Burns, J. M. (1978). Leadership. Harper & Row Publishers, N.Y, NY.

Conger, J. A. (1999). Charismatic and Transformational leadership in organizations: An insider's perspective on these developing streams of research. *Leadership Quarterly,* (pp.145–179).

Cruden's Complete Concordance to the Bible (1986). Word Aflame Press, Dugan Publishers, Inc. Gordonville, TN 38563

Dictionary by Merriam-Webster: America's most-trusted online dictionary. Retrieved from https://www.merriam-webster.com/

Dubois, W. E. B. (1903). The Talented Tenth, In T. J. Wren (Ed.), The Leaders Companion: *Insights on leadership through the ages.* Free Press. New York, N.Y.

Genetics Home Reference (April 25, 2003). The National Library of Medicine Genetics Home Reference (GHR) Retrieved from http://ghr.nlm.nih.gov/

Greenwald, R. (2010).*Today's students need leadership training like never before*: The Chronicle. Retrieved from www.chronicles.com/article/Todays-Students-Need/125604

Hopkin, Michael Ray, Leadership is a relationship, (2011). Retrieved from: https://leadonpurposeblog.com/2011/11/26/leadership-is-a-relationship/

Machiavelli, N. (1513). How Princes should keep the faith. In T. J. Wren (Ed.) (1995) The Leaders Companion: *Insights on leadership through the ages* Free Press. New York, N.Y. (p.67).

Machiavelli, N. (1984). *The prince* (Reissue ed.). Bantam. New York, NY.
New King James Version (NKJV) Copyright © 1982 by Thomas Nelson, Inc.

Plato (1901). The Republic. In J. T. Wren (Ed.), The Leader's Companion: *Insights on leadership through the ages* Free Press. New York, N.Y. (p. 60)

Publishers, Inc. and Zondervan, Wheaton, Illinois.

Schaefer, Beth (2015). University Information Technology Services, at the University of Wisconsin. Retrieved from: https://er.educause.edu/articles/2015/10/on-becoming-a-leader-building-relationships-and-creating-communities

Schenck, Kenneth (2009) *Making Sense of God's Word,* Indiana Wesleyan University; (Indianapolis: Wesleyan Publishing House, 2009).

The Application Study Bible, New International Version (NIV). (1997). Tyndale House

The University of Phoenix Material (2013) Leadership as a Reflective Praxis, Retrieved from The University of Phoenix \LDR/711A, Phoenix, Az.

Wren, J. Thomas (1995) The Leader's Companion: Insights on leadership through the ages. The Free Press, A division of Simon & Schuster Inc.,New York, NY 1002

The Holy Bible, King James Version (1990). Thomas Nelson Publishers, Inc. USA

Who's Who in the Bible (1997). Publications International, Ltd., Lincolnwood, IL 60646

PERSONAL REFLECTIONS

PERSONAL REFLECTIONS

PERSONAL REFLECTIONS

PERSONAL REFLECTIONS

PERSONAL REFLECTIONS

PERSONAL REFLECTIONS

PERSONAL REFLECTIONS

PERSONAL REFLECTIONS

PERSONAL REFLECTIONS

www.ingramcontent.com/pod-product-compliance
Lightning Source LLC
Chambersburg PA
CBHW070614010526
44118CB00012B/1509